The Life and Times of
Adelard of Bath

© 2019 Simon Webb

The right of Simon Webb to be
identified as the Author of the Work
has been asserted by him in accordance
with the Copyright, Designs
and Patents Act 1988.

All rights reserved

Published by The Langley Press, 2019

to Christiane Brown

Pictures marked 'Wellcome' are from the Wellcome Collection: https://wellcomecollection.org. Those marked 'DCC' re reprinted by kind permission of Durham County Council. Pictures marked 'Getty' are from the Getty Collection: http://www.getty.edu/art/collection. Pictures marked 'BL' are from the British Library: www.bl.uk.

The Life and Times of
Adelard of Bath

Twelfth Century
Renaissance Man

by

Simon Webb

More Books About the Middle Ages from the Langley Press

Nicholas Breakspear: The Pope from England

Aaron of Lincoln

Gilbert's Tale: The Life and Death of Thomas Becket

A Little Book of English Saints

In Search of the Celtic Saints

The Legend of St Edmund

The Life and Legend of Nicholas Flamel

In Search of Bede

The Voyage of St Brendan

In Search of St Alban

For free downloads and more from the Langley Press, please visit our website at: http://tinyurl.com/lpdirect

Contents

I. The Man on the Bridge	7
II. The Known World	13
III. The Theory of Everything	20
IV. Laon	26
V. Adelard at Antioch and Mamistra	41
VI. Italy and Sicily	48
VII. Natural Questions	54
VIII. Glimpses of a Life	61
IX. The Greatest Bathonian?	67
Bibliography	70

Detail of 19th century print of the bridge at Mamistra; now Misis in Turkey (Wellcome)

1. The Man on the Bridge

In 1114 AD a series of earthquakes hit an area equivalent to what is now the south-east of Turkey and parts of the modern states of Syria and Lebanon. There was widespread destruction: the biggest quake, which struck on the night of the twenty-ninth of November, is known to have devastated towns in the Christian County of Edessa and the Principality of Antioch – areas held by European forces since the end of the First Crusade.

The fortified town of Maras in the Principality of Antioch was almost completely destroyed, and perhaps tens of thousands of people lost their lives, including important figures such as the town's bishop, the constable and more than a hundred priests and deacons. Two important churches were demolished, and nearby villages were also reduced to rubble. A number of monasteries were also brought down by the quake, killing some of the monks.

A slightly less serious earthquake, which had struck the region some sixteen days earlier, caused some damage to a place the crusaders called Mamistra, an important port-town on the River Pyramus (now called the Ceyhan). Here there was and is an ancient stone bridge, first built during the reign of the Roman Emperor Constantius in the fourth century AD. The bridge had been restored at least twice since Constantius's time, and it needed to be re-built after the earthquakes of 1114, when it was badly shaken. The bridge at Mamistra is important in the story of Adelard of Bath because he was actually crossing the bridge when the earthquake struck.

It is thought that Adelard was born in or near the ancient English city of Bath around 1080: this would have made him about thirty-four when he found himself on a shaking bridge in Anatolia in 1114. His real name was probably 'Athelard', 'Aðelard' or something similar: it may have been changed to the more continental-looking 'Adelard' because the Anglo-Saxon letter 'eth' (ð), which gives the sound now written as 'th', looks like a 'd'. Bertrand Russell, who mentions Adelard no less than three times in his celebrated *History of Western Philosophy*, splits the difference and calls the Bathonian 'Adelhard'. In his own Latin writings, Adelard refers to himself as 'Adelardus'.

One problem with using the name 'Adelard' is that it is easily mixed up with the name of his more famous twelfth-century French contemporary Peter Abelard, who was born in 1079. He was the philosopher who fell in love with the beautiful Héloïse d'Argenteuil, incurred the wrath of her father and was brutally castrated. (Their son, Astrolabe, was named after a scientific instrument that Adelard of Bath would later write about.) Both Abelard and Adelard were scholars, and may even have met when Adelard was studying and teaching in the city of Laon in northern France, but it seems that they had quite different personalities and interests.

Although Adelard's 'real' name had an Anglo-Saxon ring to it (similar Anglo-Saxon names include Athelheah, Athelmod and Athelric) it probably cannot be said that he was a poor boy from the Anglo-Saxon underclass of Norman England, who worked his way up through sheer intelligence. The popularity of the name 'Athelard' at the time means that the evidence for this is slightly shaky, but Adelard's father was probably one Fastrad, an important tenant of Giso or Gisa, a Frenchman who had been chaplain to Edward the Confessor, and became Bishop of Wells in 1060.

When Giso died in 1088, another Frenchman, John of Tours, became bishop of Wells. John, who is also known as John of Villula, may have been the personal physician of William the Conqueror, and been by William's deathbed when he died at Rouen in 1087. In 1090 Bishop John moved the seat of his diocese from Wells to Bath: Bath Abbey had been given to him as a gift by William Rufus, son and heir of the Conqueror, and John is said to have bought the rest of the city for five hundred pounds of silver. It may be that the bishop moved his headquarters to Bath because of the wealth of the city and its abbey; but here he could also indulge his interest in medicinal bathing. He built a bath complex over the largest of Bath's hot springs, using the remains of an ancient Roman reservoir as a foundation: the King's Bath that visitors to the city see today is made up of elements from different periods, but it is thought to have been started by John of Tours. This is the bath that William Shakespeare would have known (though in an earlier form) when he visited the city, and also the bath that was known to Jane Austen and Beau Nash: the Roman bath complex here was not rediscovered until the 1870s. The evidence that Shakespeare came to Bath to try the cure can be found in his sonnets 153 and 154. In 153 he mentions:

. . . a seething bath, which yet men prove
Against strange maladies a sovereign cure.

The man from Stratford goes on to tell us that:

I, sick withal, the help of bath desired,
And thither hied, a sad distemper'd guest,
But found no cure: the bath for my help lies
Where Cupid got new fire; my mistress' eyes.

The idea is repeated in sonnet 154:

. . . I, my mistress' thrall,
Came there for cure, and this by that I prove,
Love's fire heats water, water cools not love.

The sonnets quoted above suggest that Shakespeare sought a cure for some sexually transmitted disease, but the hot springs were also supposed to supply an effective treatment for leprosy (now known as Hansen's disease). Bladud, the legendary founder of Bath, is said to have been banished from the royal court because he had become a leper. He survived by taking up the profession of swineherd, but unfortunately he transmitted his leprosy to his pigs. One day, however, they found a hot spring in a remote spot near Keynsham, and wallowed in the waters. This cured them and, when Bladud followed suit, the waters healed him as well. Bladud's royal status was restored, and he went on to found Bath, build a bath complex in the city, become King Bladud, and father another legendary prince of the Britons, King Lear. A seventeenth-century statue of Bladud can still be seen overlooking the King's Bath.

Various skin diseases were supposed to respond well to the Bath treatment, and late in the twelfth century the scholar-abbot Alexander Neckam wrote that they gave strength to the weak, and youth to the aged. Neckam also speculated about how the waters were heated underground before they rose to the surface, imagining huge brass pots under the earth. He also asserted that the waters gave off the odour of sanctity as well as the smells of sulphur, cinnamon, cassia and myrrh. In his Latin poem *De laudibus divinæ sapientiæ* (*In Praise of Divine Wisdom*) Neckam attributes the success of the baths at Bath as a medical treatment to their combination of nature and human art: nature provided the hot water, people built the bath.

Although Adelard would not have seen the Roman baths, he would have seen John of Tours' baths, and the old Roman forum, which was still a conspicuous feature of the city in the twelfth century.

The current value (in 2019) of five thousand pounds weight of silver is somewhat over ninety thousand UK pounds Stirling: it may be that Bishop John got a bargain when he bought Bath for that sum, but we should bear in mind that the whole city is supposed to have been burned down during a rebellion against William Rufus in 1088, when Adelard would have been perhaps eight years old.

As a local boy, Adelard would have witnessed changes beyond the destruction of the city and the building of the first version of the King's Bath by Bishop John. As part of his commitment to the city as the new seat of his diocese, John rebuilt the church, giving the city a large church that no longer survives: the present Bath

Abbey is much smaller. The man from Tours also gave the monks of Bath an impressive library, and founded a priory. It may be that some of this development was made easier by the fact that much if not all of the city had recently been razed to the ground. The total destruction of a city, sometimes preceded by looting and accompanied by violence against the citizens, was a popular tactic of twelfth century armies.

A local boy who wanted an education could hardly have done better at that time than to have attached himself to John of Tours. Although he is not supposed to have been very learned himself, and spoke so badly that even children laughed at him, Bishop John turned Bath into an important seat of learning, and a contemporary document records that one Aðelhardus was a *dapifer* or steward in the bishop's household in 1100. It may be that Bishop John's personal sponsorship, together with Adelard's family's connections to the diocese, are what enabled the Bathonian to pursue such an expensive education, and even to seek knowledge outside of Europe.

In the twelfth century in western Europe, knowledge and education were very much in the hands of the Church. Very few women could read or write, and a man who could do so was almost by definition a churchman, especially if he could read and write Latin. Latin was widely used by scholars, which meant that students and teachers like Adelard could transfer to schools in continental Europe without having any language problems. The cathedral schools of the time followed a curriculum based around the Seven Liberal Arts – Grammar, Logic, Rhetoric, Arithmetic, Geometry, Astronomy and Music. In his book *On the Same and the Different* Adelard suggested that the Seven Arts had appeared, in the remote past, by a kind of miracle, to help people make sense of the world. The knowledge and skills students acquired while studying these were of course useful far beyond the Church itself. Scholars often found themselves working for kings and lesser magnates, advising on such subjects as accounting, astrology, diplomacy and architecture.

As a scholar, Adelard is particularly associated with the twelfth-century growth in interest in the so-called Quadrivium: the last four of the Seven Liberal Arts listed above. Arithmetic, Geometry, Astronomy and Music are rather more scientific in character than the Trivium, the first three subjects; Grammar, Logic and Rhetoric. This contemporary widening of academic interests, and the general growth and improvement in learning at the time tempted the American historian C.H. Haskins to coin the term 'Twelfth Century Renaissance' and to publish a book on the subject in 1927. Haskins wrote that the period saw such exciting developments as:

the beginnings of Gothic art; the emergence of vernacular literatures; the revival of the Latin classics and of Latin poetry and Roman law; the recovery of Greek science, with its Arabic additions, and of much of Greek philosophy; and the origin of the first European universities.

As we shall see, Adelard of Bath, who is not well-known even in the city of Bath itself, was a key figure in Haskins' renaissance. What made him unique among his fellow twelfth-century renaissance men and women was his focus on the 'Arabic additions' to the science of the ancients.

11. The Known World

Although Haskins identified the twelfth century as 'in many respects an age of fresh and vigorous life', the scholars of the age had an attachment to the past which modern scientists in particular might find excessive, even obsessive. Ideas were hardly valued unless they could be proved to have some connection to the ancient world – in many ways this was a *re-birth* of knowledge, not a new birth.

Thinkers in the twelfth century had so much respect for the science, culture and particularly the philosophy of the ancient Greeks and Romans that figures such as the contemporary Jewish scholar Maimonides, whose life overlapped with Adelard's, felt compelled to try to reconcile his modern Jewish religion with ancient pagan thought. Although careful observation of the heavens would have debunked it, the astronomers of the period also still adhered to a model of the universe that put the earth at the centre of everything – a model attributed to the Egyptian Claudius Ptolemy, who died over nine hundred years before Adelard was born.

Although they understood that the earth was round, and speculated about what lay to the far east and west of Europe, the known world, for Adelard and most of his European contemporaries, meant Europe, North Africa and parts of the Middle East. They were aware of the existence of India, but their knowledge of the East often grew very misty east of what we now call Turkey.

Most of the modern state of Turkey is made up of Anatolia,

also known as Asia Minor, which lies between the Black Sea and the Eastern Mediterranean. Anatolia was the location of many famous cities, some of which will be familiar to readers acquainted with the New Testament. The modern names of these places are all Turkish: their ancient names included Tarsus in Cilicia, which was very near to Mamistra, and was the birth-place of St Paul. Other such names included Ephesus, Pergamon, Smyrna, Mitylene, Nicomedia and Seleucia.

After the Battle of Manzikert in 1071 the Turks were able to take over most of Anatolia, forcing back the Byzantine Empire, the remaining portion of the ancient Roman Empire. The Eastern Empire was now limited to the area of modern Greece, plus some territories, such as Macedonia and Albania, beyond modern Greece's north-western border. The Byzantines also continued to hold some pockets of land around the Black Sea coasts, and Mediterranean islands such as Crete, Rhodes and Cyprus.

Around 1092, when Adelard was a boy of about twelve years old, Anatolia would not have been the only place in the known world that had once been dominated by Christians, but had been taken over by Muslims. Much of what we now know as Spain and Portugal then comprised the Muslim territory of Al-Andalus. The Mediterranean coast of Africa was also dominated by Islam.

Nobody living through the twelfth century renaissance would have called the new cultural flowering a 'renaissance' – the term only came into use in the nineteenth century. Many of Adelard's contemporaries would also have been forgiven for thinking that their century was not about cultural flowering at all – as the tragic experience of Adelard's near-namesake Peter Abelard makes clear, there was a great deal of brutality in evidence, and many of those who were not blessed with Adelard's good luck lived short lives of unimaginable harshness, unrelieved by any meaningful glimpses of knowledge.

Some of the most significant developments of Adelard's life-time were born out of ignorance, prejudice and cruelty rather than enlightenment. Undoubtedly the most important event in Adelard's known world was the First Crusade. In my Church of England primary school in the 1960s I was taught that the Crusades started when thousands of brave Christian knights, inspired by a speech from the Pope, marched east to Jerusalem and won back that holy city for Jesus (I cannot recall their being a single Muslim in the school). In reality, the First Crusade was a much more complex phenomenon. It is likely that the recent loss of Anatolia was uppermost in the minds of many of the Crusaders who set off in 1095, and it is certain that many of them were inspired by the prospect of personal gain rather than any 'sacred mission' to force the Muslims out of the Holy Land.

As described by the chronicler Peter the Monk, Pope Urban II's Crusade-launching speech at Clermont in France in November 1095 was a classic piece of rabble-rousing. According to Urban, the wicked 'Persians' who had invaded the Holy Land were overturning Christian altars, defecating on them, forcibly circumcising Christians and smearing the resulting blood on the church plate. When the mood took them, they would also kill Christians by slowly pulling out their bowels, and they treated Christian women so badly that Urban hesitated to mention what the actually did. Now, said the Pope, these foreigners had 'dismembered' the Greek Empire, capturing an area so large that it could not be traversed in two months.

Urban urged his listeners to recapture the martial glory of their ancestors and march east out of lands that, he asserted, could no longer support them in any case. Now was the time to put aside petty squabbles and local wars, and to rescue Jerusalem, the 'navel of the world'. Peter the Monk tells us that Urban's listeners responded by repeating the cry, 'God wills it!' This became a war-cry for the Crusaders.

The problem with rabble-rousing speeches is that they tend to rouse rabbles. Even the crusading parties that set off in good order soon became undisciplined rabbles, looting and pillaging whenever supplies ran low, or greed got the better of them. Infected with a particularly virulent form of religious mania, some paused to massacre Jews along the way. Among these anti-Semites was the Frenchman Peter the Hermit (not to be confused with the aforementioned Peter the Monk). Peter assembled and led the disastrous People's Crusade: many of the unarmed peasants he attempted to march to Jerusalem never made it out of Europe: most of those who got as far as Anatolia were massacred at the Battle of Civetot near Nicaea in 1096. The battle was in the north-west of Anatolia – Peter's peasants had not marched very far beyond Constantinople, the Byzantine capital.

The First Crusade had been inspired in part by messages from Alexius I, the then Byzantine Emperor, begging the Pope and the western or Latin Christian kingdoms for help against the Turks. Our best source on Emperor Alexius is the *Alexiad*, a biography written by the emperor's daughter Anna Comnena, a near-contemporary of Adelard of Bath. Anna describes in great detail the problems Alexius and his empire faced when waves of Crusaders began passing through his territories. The Emperor tried to keep these new arrivals on his side by offering them practical and monetary assistance, and persuading many of them to swear oaths of allegiance to himself. But the Latin Christians, whom Anna often calls 'Keltoi', meaning 'Celts', proved to be very hard to control, and the *Alexiad* contains many accounts of desperate battles between Byzantine imperial forces and Crusaders. At the same time, Anna's father had to deal with continuing attacks from the Turks, and rebellions, desertions, defections and attempts at palace coups that originated among his own people.

As was usually the case in the twelfth century, religion had a large part to play in these conflicts. Yes, the Byzantines and the Latin Christians were supposed to share a religion, but each regarded the other side as heretical. The Christians of the West used Latin in their liturgy, and followed the Pope, supposedly an apostolic descendant of St Peter. The Byzantines used Greek, and so much authority over their church was vested in the emperor that Alexius's daughter Anna Comnena describes episodes where her father intervened in conflicts over dogma by meeting supposed heretics and giving them lectures about what they were supposed to believe.

The activities of Bohemond, one of the leaders of the First Crusade, must have seemed particularly alarming to Alexius and his supporters. Indeed, the Emperor's heart must have sunk when he first learned that Bohemond was joining the Crusade.

Bohemond was a member of a terrifying Norman family, the de Hautevilles, who had taken over the whole of Sicily and Southern Italy, and had even attempted to invade Byzantine Albania in 1082. The Emperor Alexius had fought against Bohemond himself in that campaign, and the sense that Bohemond was determined to use the First Crusade as an opportunity to take over new territories in the East was so strong that the English chronicler William of Malmesbury, a younger contemporary of Adelard's, was convinced that the Crusade had been cooked up merely to satisfy Bohemond's territorial ambitions.

Anna Comnena described Bohemond as a man quite unlike any who had been seen before by her people. Standing over cubit taller than any other man, the warlike Norman was powerfully built, with yellow hair, blue eyes and a chin as smooth and hairless as marble. The clean-shaven look of Bohemond and some of the other Crusaders was disconcerting to the Byzantine Greeks, who considered beards an essential part of manhood.

Despite his imposing appearance, Anna detected a certain charm about the Norman, who also seemed decisive and well-informed. History records that power accumulated around Bohemond in a way that seems almost mysterious. He inspired confidence, which was often misplaced, and had a tendency to take charge of things when technically he had no right to do so.

Bohemond's Nordic appearance would have made this blond giant stand out among the smaller, darker Byzantines: he could hardly have blended in with many Frenchmen either. His startling look was a reminder of the Scandinavian origins of the Normans, who were literally the 'north men' who had came south into France in search of land and loot.

From October 1097, Bohemond expended a lot of time and energy on the siege of Antioch. The siege was an example of how he could find himself running an operation, although it was supposed to be in the hands of someone else entirely. The Norman finally won the city in May 1098, thus founding the Crusader state of the Principality of Antioch, which survived for one hundred and seventy years. Bohemond's story has a bearing on the life of Adelard, because it is likely that Norman Antioch was one of the places in the East that was visited by the man from Bath.

Although the armies of the time did fight battles at sea and in the open field, a lot of time was spent on siege warfare. Anna Comnena's *Alexiad* is full of accounts of armies settling down before fortified towns and cities and setting about getting through the walls by deception, or bribery, or the use of blockades and siege engines, some of which were based on technology inherited from the ancient Romans. In his account of the twelfth century earthquakes in the area, Nicholas Ambraseys suggests that the Crusader areas may have been particularly badly hit because many of the castles and city walls had been hastily repaired after prolonged battering during a siege. Other castles collapsed because they had been rapidly built from scratch on hills that were severely shaken by the quakes (see bibliography for details of Ambraseys' work).

Time and again, the Byzantines did well in such confrontations because of their use of Greek fire, a medieval technology that meant that, in effect, they had flame-throwers at their disposal. The masts and rigging of enemy ships approaching Byzantine ports, such as Constantinople itself, would suddenly burst into flames, as a dragon-like tongue of fire reached across the water. Ingenious siege-towers would likewise be reduced to ashes before they could even be wheeled into position, and Anna Comnena gives an account of a sea-battle between the Byzantines and the Pisans, where the Greeks were able to vomit fire from the prows of their ships.

Bohemond's ambitions in the East went far beyond the possession of a mere Crusader state, hemmed in by other Crusader states, the Armenians in Cilicia, the Turks, and the Eastern Mediterranean. He saw the wily, resourceful Emperor Alexius as the main barrier between himself and the possession of much larger territories, and he returned to Italy and launched an ill-advised invasion of Byzantine Albania, as his father Robert Guiscard had done over twenty years earlier. Alexius's wily strategy soon left Bohemond stranded and helpless, and he had to submit to a humiliating peace. He died just three years later, in 1111, but at least he was able to leave Antioch to his descendants, together with his possessions in Southern Italy.

The Norman takeovers of England, Sicily and Southern Italy, and the Turkish gains in the East, had changed the map of Adelard's known world in the decades before his birth. The First Crusade changed things again when Adelard was a teenager and a young man. The Turks had been pushed back, albeit temporarily; there were Latin Christian strongholds in Asia, and Jerusalem itself had fallen into Western hands. Napoleon said that you could tell a lot about a man, based on what the world was like when he was twenty. When Adelard of Bath was twenty, the world seemed to offer intriguing new opportunities to an adventurous young scholar.

III. The Theory of Everything

Adelard's encounter with seismic forces on the bridge at Mamistra in 1114 is one of a series of striking incidents in his life that he himself relates in his writings. The problem for the biographer of Adelard is that, because of the conventions of twelfth century literature, Adelard may have invented some of these incidents merely to make a point and to add interest to his pages: they may not actually have happened in any real sense, and worse, the Bathonian may never have been to some of the places he claims to have visited.

As a student, Adelard probably did spend time at Tours in France: this was, after all, the original home of the man who may have acted as his patron – John of Tours, the Bishop of Bath. One adventure Adelard claimed to have met with in Tours cannot, however, have been real, although in his Latin text *De eodem et diverso* (*On the Same and the Different*) he presents it as if it was.

On the Same and the Different is couched in the form of a message to an unnamed nephew of Adelard's. Confusingly, it is also dedicated to William, the Bishop of Syracuse in Sicily, of whom more later. The book, which takes up about thirty-five pages in English translation, is supposed to have been written as a reply to a complaint of the author's nephew, who questioned his uncle's habit of studying hard and travelling to different parts of the world to do so. *On the Same and the Different* relates an imaginary, symbolic encounter Adelard is supposed to have experienced one night as a student by the River Loire at Tours.

He tells us that he was outside looking at the stars with a wise, unnamed teacher, who was explaining them to him. Eventually the teacher, who was older than Adelard, announced that he was going home, but suggested that the young Englishman stay behind and consider for himself whether what he, the teacher, had said was true.

Alone by the river under the stars, Adelard was met by two groups of female figures, who were all personifications. Such figures are very common in medieval literature, including drama, but we moderns are more likely to be familiar with them from old statues and paintings. The Statue of Liberty in New York is a good example of a personification of freedom: the figure of Britannia on English bank-notes, with her spear and shield, is supposed to embody or personify some idea of the British nation.

Adelard's two parties of female personifications were led by Philosophia and Philocosmia respectively. 'Philosophia' or 'philosophy' literally means 'love of wisdom'; 'Philocosmia' is supposed to personify love of the world.

As if to show that she was part of a tableau that had both sound and vision, Philocosmia began to address Adelard. Since she represented the opposite of the love of wisdom, she criticised the Bathonian's quest for knowledge. Why did he spend so much time looking for answers which, when he found them, only gave rise to more questions? He should listen to her advice and seek after the pleasures offered by her alluring female followers. These ladies included Riches: her adherents possessed gold, silver, jewels, large, fertile lands and an enviable measure of contentment. People think the rich are wiser than the philosophers, who are so poor that they beg in streets. The philosophers are not content, and are always disagreeing with each other, pecking away at each other like magpies.

Philocosmia also sets out the attractions of Power, who is respected everywhere, and Honour, who is even sought out by the philosophers, and is the key to landing powerful administrative jobs. A fourth maiden, Fame, is covered with feathers and eyes: she drove heroes like Jason to perform seemingly impossible deeds, and she can confer immortality. Finally Pleasure herself rules the senses, and forms the basis of the Epicurean philosophy.

On her side, Philosophia is attended by our friends the Seven Liberal Arts. Grammar holds a book covered in corrections, and Rhetoric is dressed in clothing with whatever can be debated woven into it. Dialectic also holds a book, containing ten distinctions. In her other hand, she holds a serpent, and Philosophia explains how useful Dialectic is in making sense of things. Arithmetic wears a cloak woven with numbers, and Music holds a cymbal in one hand, and a music-book in the other. Philosophia describes how powerful music is, how it attracts people, and how a sense of music is instilled in tiny children by their nurses, who sing to them to calm them down.

In this section on music, Adelard inserts one of his tantalizing autobiographical snapshots. Philosophia reminds him how, when he was studying music in France, a queen asked the Bathonian to play the cittern for her. The sounds he produced on this lute-like instrument inspired a little boy to move his hands and fingers in time to the music, provoking much laughter.

Like his experience on the bridge at Mamistra, and the other glimpses of his life that Adelard gives us, what we might call the 'cittern incident' raises more questions than it answers. Who was this queen? Was she French? Did this happen at Tours, or Laon, or elsewhere in France?

At the end of *On the Same and the Different* Philosophia introduces Adelard to the last two personifications of the Seven Liberal Arts – Geometry and Astronomy. The author was to write more about these: he translated an Arabic version of Euclid's *Elements*, the archetypal textbook of geometry, into Latin, and he also wrote a treatise on the astrolabe – an ancient astronomical instrument that had been much improved by the Arabs.

Of course Adelard allows Philosophia to defeat Philocosmia during their encounter by the River Loire. The odds are, after all, heavily weighted against Philocosmia, who speaks first, has fewer hand-maidens to assist her, and is given less time to speak. The book fulfils its purpose of countering Adelard's nephew's objection to his uncle's habit of wandering all over the world in pursuit of new studies. Philocosmia explains how wisdom can rein in the enthusiasms of youth, and bring comfort in old age, and she goes on to reveal that different countries are better at different elements of learning, so that the student who finds France deficient in one area should travel to Italy and even Greece. As we know, Adelard went even further east than that.

The map of knowledge that Philocosmia describes, where different parts of the world have different specialisations, is compared by her to the human body. Not all the organs can do everything – even the brain is divided into three parts, the front being the seat of the imagination, in front of reason, with memory at the back. This use of the human body as a metaphor is reminiscent of a saying of Adelard's younger contemporary, Nicholas Breakspear, who became the only English pope to date. Answering a question about the wealth of the Church posed by his fellow-Englishman John of Salisbury, Nicholas, who took the name of Adrian IV when he assumed Peter's chair, said that the Church was like the stomach, that takes all the food, but distributes its goodness to all the other parts of the body.

Winding up his *On the Same and the Different*, Adelard gives us another of his autobiographical flashes. He asserts that, having witnessed Philosophia shaming Philocosmia into defeat, he was inspired to redouble his efforts as a student, and travel further afield in search of knowledge. He tells us that, leaving the Italian city of Salerno, he encountered a Greek philosopher in Magna Graecia, a region of Italy that had once been part of the Byzantine Empire, but was ruled by the Normans when Adelard was there. This unnamed man, who (if he ever existed) presumably embodied the wisdom of both the Latins and the Greeks, taught Adelard about medicine and 'the nature of things'. He tested his student's wisdom, and, in a reflective moment, told Adelard that one never regretted studying the Liberal Arts, which, for him, enhanced the pleasures of his quiet moments. In fact, the mysterious Greek confided in Adelard that he sometimes wished that, as a young man, he had studied more.

The anonymous Greek-Italian sage who appears at the end of Adelard's *On the Same and the Different* seems rather similar to the unnamed teacher the Bathonian mentions at the beginning of the same book. This suggests that, like Philosophia, Philocosmia and their attendants, these two sages are people Adelard just made up to give a satisfying shape to his narrative.

It would seem from Adelard's later book, *Natural Questions*, that the Bathonian's nephew did apply himself to his studies, though he continued to have reservations about his uncle's wandering ways. Whether he was inspired by *On the Same and the Different* to study harder is unclear. What is certain is that *On the Same and the Different* is a well-structured, well-judged argument in favour of knowledge, and a brief, coherent and effective summary of knowledge as it was understood by twelfth century European scholars. The author draws on the ideas of Plato, Aristotle, Pythagoras, Boethius and others, but also uses examples from his own experience, and from experiences common to everyone. To show how what we might now call 'sensory input' can distract the mind from reasonable decision-making, for instance, he recalls how people often seek out a quiet, lonely place to think over important issues.

The work's title, *On the Same and the Different*, has to do with some of the contemporary philosophical ideas that underlie the text. Adelard implies that philosophy, which he sets against mere thoughtless sensual engagement with the world, has a tendency to find connections between things, and to seek out unifying patterns. By contrast Philocosmia, love of the world, tends to split things apart and emphasise their differences. The medieval philosophers' quest for the unity of Creation is reminiscent of the current search for the elusive Theory of Everything, an idea in physics that, potentially, could explain why the whole universe is the way it is.

A theory of the whole universe that tantalized thinkers of Adelard's generation had been put forward by the Greek philosopher Plato. It had to do with what some called 'universals', the abstract, general 'ideas' of things, which Plato suggested were more real than the things themselves. Since the unnamed Greek sage that Adelard met is described as having knowledge on 'the nature of things' we must assume, given the twelfth-century context, that Adelard and his mentor discussed the vexed question of 'universals'.

'Universals' have to do with the relationship between things themselves, the names of things, and their true natures. Remember how Anna Comnena described the Nordic giant Bohemond as quite unlike any man who had ever been seen in her part of the world. We have no reason to doubt her assertion – but we can also be sure that, despite his outlandish appearance, Anna's fellow-countrymen would have been able to identify the Norman Crusader as a man, without any hesitation. This suggests that people carry about in their heads an abstract, general idea of a man which, among other things, helps them to identify a man when they come across one. People must have similar general, abstract ideas of many other things stored away in their brains – rivers, bridges, cities, earthquakes.

To Plato, these ideas or universals were so real that they made the versions of them that are perceived by the senses mere illusions – no more real than shadows or reflections. Although the medieval Christian scholars revered Plato, they found that his approach to 'universals' was hard to reconcile with the Christian conception of Creation. This difficulty led to many prolonged and complex disputes, with some saying, for instance, that 'universals' were nothing more than mere words. In Adelard's *On the Same and the Different*, Philocosmia satirises the behaviour of Philosophia's followers, endlessly picking over irrelevant questions about things and universals, adhering to fleeting theories while they descended into poverty and become ragged beggars.

Adelard included his own approach to the question of universals in his *On the Same and the Different*. He asserted that a thing, such as a man, contained the idea of a man within itself, so that, to use our example of Bohemond, the warrior contained within himself enough of the general, abstract, universal idea of a man to be recognised as a man. This seems more like a useful observation than a solution to the problem of universals, but it is worthwhile all the same. Unlike the universals of Plato, that the philosopher suggested dwelt as real entities in the mind of God, the signs of universals Adelard detected in things themselves were features that could be observed by a scientifically-minded man like the Bathonian.

IV. Laon

In keeping with his professed determination to travel to study, Adelard learned and taught not only in Tours, but further north in France, at Laon.

For a period of about twenty years, the cathedral school at Laon was included with Paris and Chartres in the list of the three most prestigious centres of learning in Western Europe. It was here that Adelard may have met his contemporary and near-namesake, Peter Abelard, and we can get a picture of what life was like for scholars there from Abelard's short autobiography, the *Historia Calamitatum* or 'History of [My] Calamities', which he wrote around 1132.

Abelard tells us that he was lured to Laon by the prospect of being taught by Anselm of Laon, a native of the place who had won a great reputation for himself as a scholar. This Anselm, who should not be confused with his better-known contemporary Saint Anselm of Canterbury, was probably in his early sixties when Abelard arrived in 1113.

The older man's teaching did not impress Abelard, who found him lacking in brains and insight. Anselm spoke well, but what he said seemed to make no sense to Abelard. He was the mere shadow of a great man, or like a man who starts a fire but only makes smoke. When people asked him questions, Abelard writes, Anselm's answers only made them more confused.

Abelard started to attend Anselm's lectures less and less, and, as a man who easily made enemies, he soon found that his fellow-students were whispering about him to Anselm. Their plan was to persuade the master to hate his new student, and to this end one of the whisperers asked Abelard what he thought of the lectures on Scripture that he had heard at Laon. This was at an informal meeting of scholars, after a lecture, when there seems to have been a lot of banter going back and forth.

Seldom hesitant about making a bold statement or giving an audacious answer, Abelard claimed that any educated person could understand the Scriptures just by reading them, together with a few glosses. Lectures on this subject might be good for the soul, but otherwise they were quite unnecessary. Abelard's fellow-students scoffed at this outrageous assertion, and challenged him to lecture to them on any Biblical passage of their choosing. Abelard accepted, and they saddled him with a very obscure passage from the Old Testament Book of Ezekiel. Abelard invited them to his lecture on that passage, which he proposed to give *the very next day*.

A film-maker, tacking this scene, might make the sound-track go very quiet at this point. The film might cut to a shot including the back of Abelard's head, with the hushed scholars gazing in amazement at his unseen face. One of the scholars, perhaps Adelard of Bath himself, suddenly pale to the roots of his hair, steps forward. 'Tomorrow? Peter, you mustn't think of doing it so soon. You're like me – you've only ever studied the sciences. You must allow yourself some more time . . .'

'Nonsense,' Abelard replies. 'I am accustomed to doing well because of my innate talent, not by dint of long periods of study. I will not give my lecture at all unless you agree to come to it tomorrow.'

The next shot is bathed in yellow morning light. We hear a cock crow as Peter Abelard, bright-eyed, bushy-tailed and wearing a confident smile, walks into a room where a select band of scholars has assembled to hear him.

According to Abelard, his first lecture on the Scriptures was a great success. Word spread, and the Laon scholars demanded more of the same, and avidly copied the notes others had made at the first lecture, on that tough passage in Ezekiel.

But the whisperers who were determined to set Anselm against

Abelard continued their work, and soon Anselm himself and two other leading teachers – Alberic of Rheims and Lotulphe the Lombard – were insisting that Abelard abandon his lectures on the Scriptures. If Abelard should make serious mistakes due to his inexperience, Anselm argued, then the blame might fall on me.

Although something similar had happened at Paris, where Abelard had clashed with his master, William of Champeaux, Abelard now returned to Paris and won fame and some fortune with his lectures on Ezekiel. Soon, however, the ill-fated affair between himself and his beautiful and brilliant young student Héloïse began to write itself into history.

The story of Abelard's time at Laon shows how different the cathedral schools of the twelfth century were from today's universities. Whereas today some struggling students might pay for extra, private tuition from freelance tutors, it was then possible for a charismatic figure like Abelard to breeze in and lure paying customers away from the established masters of the place. Whether Adelard of Bath was ever tempted to sample Peter Abelard's audacious teaching at Laon or elsewhere is not known – he never mentions the Frenchman in his writings. It is unlikely, however, that the Bathonian was not aware of Peter Abelard, if he really was at Laon at the same time as his more famous contemporary.

Since Adelard never mentions Abelard, even when he is writing about his time at Laon, it is possible that the two men did not coincide there. If they did, it is likely that their different social circles and academic interests kept them apart. At the time, Laon had strong links to England, and Adelard might have been tempted to spend time with his fellow-countrymen, much as, for instance, Australians attending modern-day English universities might seek each other out and form an Australian 'society' in their college. In any case Adelard may not have been particularly interested in Abelard's lectures on Ezekiel because he was too engrossed in the teaching of Anselm of Laon's brother, Ralph. While Anselm concentrated on teaching theology, Ralph is supposed to have taught everything else.

Of particular interest in relation to Adelard of Bath's possible later career is the fact that Ralph wrote a book on the abacus. This was not the familiar Chinese abacus or counting-frame, but a system for making arithmetical calculations using numbered counters on a grid either drawn in sand or mapped out on a tablecloth. Ralph of Laon's book on the abacus is particularly interesting because his system employed a zero – in his case a circle with a dot in the middle, which he called 'sipos'. Although the system Ralph described is basically no more complex than that used by a child in a modern primary school to add, subtract or multiply using a pencil and paper, it was cutting-edge new technology in twelfth century Western Europe. It was of such interest to Adelard that he wrote his own treatise on the abacus.

As R. L. Poole suggests in his book *The Twelfth Century Exchequer*, an important secondary source for Adelard's life, Adelard may have been the man, or one of the men, who introduced the use of the abacus into the English Treasury. Certainly this innovation would not have been the first or only learned idea that made its way from Laon to Norman England. Poole mentions two Englishmen who were bishops of Laon, two bishops of English sees who were educated there, and a future Archbishop of Canterbury who had lived and taught at Laon. When the cathedral burned down in 1112, priests from Laon were sent all over Europe begging for money to re-build it. When a party of them reached England in 1123, they found that their city's reputation for learning had preceded them wherever they went, and that many Laon alumni were willing to put their hands in their pockets to help the old place out.

It is unlikely that Adelard of Bath ever made himself as conspicuous at Laon as Peter Abelard did during his brief time there. We know that he had his own students, as well as studying in his own right, and that the nephew who features in three of his written works was among them; but this does not mean that, like Peter Abelard, he was lecturing to larger and larger audiences and challenging the masters of the place with his popularity. In his *Natural Questions* Adelard tells us that it was at Laon that he left his students to continue their studies, while he set off for seven years of study among the Arabs. Whether Adelard only travelled for seven years, and exactly when all this happened, is unclear; but if we accept that the Bathonian was on the bridge at Mamistra when the earthquake struck in 1114, then we must also accept that he was on his travels by then. The problem is that we don't know where he went before and after Mamistra, how long he stayed there, or whether he was heading east over the bridge and getting further away from home, or heading west back into Europe.

It is likely that he was out of England, if not Europe, for far longer than the seven years he is supposed to have spent in the East. Long sojourns in France and Italy would not have been unusual for a well set-up scholar at the time.

Even today, in our globalized twenty-first century world, it would be unusual for an English scholar who was not a Muslim and had no Middle-Eastern ethnicity to set out to study in the Islamic world. Why did Adelard head east? To many western European scholars of the twelfth century, the question would have seemed foolish.

For modern people in the West, the problem is that we still view Islam through post-colonial spectacles, and find it hard to recapture the high intellectual kudos the Arabs enjoyed all around the Mediterranean world as Europe emerged from the Dark Ages. Within living memory, millions of Muslims lived under the heel of the British Empire, and the western powers continue to meddle in the affairs of sovereign nations in the Middle East. In the nineteenth and early twentieth centuries, the Arabs were often seen as backward, lazy, superstitious and untrustworthy. Today many in the West only associate Muslims with terrorism and religious fanaticism.

The Western sense that the people of the East may be inferior, even flawed, in comparison to the western people who were briefly their masters is beautifully summed up in a passage in the 1943 children's story *The Little Prince*, by the French writer Antoine de Saint-Exupéry. In this passage, we are told about a fictional asteroid called B-216. This was spotted by a Turkish astronomer in 1909, who presented his findings to an international conference of astronomers. Nobody believed him, because he was wearing Turkish costume. When he tried exactly the same presentation again at another conference eleven years later, in Western costume, his findings were accepted. 'Grown-ups are like that' explains the narrator of *The Little Prince*.

By the time Adelard of Bath started to take an interest in Arabic culture, the West already owed a great debt to Muslim science, especially in the field of astronomy, where Saint-Exupéry's fictional Turkish professor made his discovery. We have already mentioned the astrolabe, an ancient scientific instrument which the Arabs greatly improved. At least one gleaming example of an astrolabe always seems to be on display in any oriental museum in the West, or in any gallery devoted to Islamic culture in the world's great museums. These remarkable instruments could take months to build, because the makers had to calculate exactly where to engrave the numbers, symbols and marks that can be seen all over them. The Saphaea, an improved type of astrolabe, was invented by the Spanish Moslem astronomer Al-Zarkali, who died when Adelard was around seven years of age. Al-Zarkali also produced his own Book of Tables, a type of almanac that allowed the reader to work out the date according to various different calendars, and also to predict eclipses and the future positions of the planets.

Al-Zarkali built on the work of the ninth-century Persian scholar al-Khwarizmi, who was interested in mathematics as well as astronomy. He gave us the word 'algebra' and his name was adapted into the word 'algorithm'. Latin translations of al-Khwarizmi's works on arithmetic, including one attributed to Adelard of Bath, popularised the use of so-called 'Arabic numerals' in the West: al-Khwarizmi himself called these 'Indian' numbers.

Both al-Khwarizmi and al-Zarkali corrected and improved on the work of the aforementioned Claudius Ptolemy, whose Earth-centred model of the universe was the dominant one at the time. Their work is just one example of what Haskins identified as the 'Arabic additions' to the ideas of the ancient Greeks and Romans. Since the original Greek and Latin versions of the works of many of these ancient experts had been lost by the twelfth century, the only way they could be reintroduced into the West was via translations from Arabic into Latin. It was possible to do such work by learning Arabic at home and acquiring Arabic texts by what we might call mail-order. But Adelard of Bath, who may already have been fluent in Arabic by the time he set off for the East, evidently preferred to get his Arabic learning from somewhere closer to the source.

*Abelard and Heloise, from an early
15th century manuscript (Getty)*

Philosophy presenting the Seven Liberal Arts to Boethius, from a 15th century manuscript (Getty). The 6th century Roman philosopher Boethius inspired some aspects of Adelard's book On the Same and the Different.

A falcon, from a late 13th century manuscript. Adelard's treatise of falconry included advice on training these birds, and treating their various illnesses (BL)

Albertus Magnus teaching. Albertus put Adelard's Liber Prestigiorum *at the top of his list of 'abominable' books (Wellcome)*

*Greek, Latin and Arab notaries in Sicily, from
a book by Peter of Eboli (DCC)*

*18th century print showing the ruins of
ancient Antioch (Wellcome)*

An astrolabe (Wellcome). Adelard wrote a manual for this ancient scientific instrument, which was greatly improved by the Arabs. Astrolabes were used for astronomy and navigation, among other things

Claudius Ptolemy and Euclid, on either side of a depiction of Ptolemy's idea of the universe, with the Earth at the centre. Adelard produced a ground-breaking Latin translation of an Arabic version of Euclid's Elements *(Wellcome)*

Al-Edrisi's world map (DCC)

Illuminations from British Library manuscript Burney 275: a 14th century French book including texts by Adelard. Geometry and Astronomy

V. Adelard at Antioch and Mamistra

It is thought that, during his travels outside of Europe, the Bathonian spent time in the aforementioned Crusader Principality of Antioch. When he crossed the shaky bridge at Mamistra in 1114, he could have been on his way there, or returning from there, perhaps using one of the routes across Anatolia that the First Crusaders had used.

Antioch was another of those ancient cities, the site of which is now in the modern state of Turkey. The city is mentioned twenty-one times in the Bible, all of these references being in the New Testament, but none in the Gospels. The majority of New Testament mentions are in the Book of Acts, which tells the story of the fledgling Christian Church after the Ascension of Jesus. Only two references to Antioch are in the New Testament letters (Galatians 2:11 and 2 Timothy 3:11).

The story of the first Christians in Antioch is part of the story of how the Gospel began to spread beyond the Holy Land around the edges of the Mediterranean, into Greek-speaking cities that had once been part of the Greek Empire. In the days of St Peter and St Paul, many of these cities were ruled from Rome. Some of their citizens would have been Jews at this time, and in fact the first mention of Antioch in the New Testament (Acts 6:5) concerns one Nicholas from Antioch, a convert to Judaism who became an important Christian in the very early days. The proud boast of Antioch is that it was here that the early followers of Jesus were first called 'Christians' (Acts 11:26).

Antioch lay on the River Orontes, which allowed the

Antiochenes access to the Mediterranean via the port of Seleucia. By the eleventh century, the harbour at Seleucia had silted up, so traders sent their goods by pack-animals across land to the newer port of St Simeon. These goods included gold, silver, rich fabrics and jewels.

The Orontes also served Antioch as a defensive moat to the west, while Mount Silpius overshadowed the city from the east, making invasion from that direction very difficult. An Arab Christian doctor called Ibn Butlan, who came to Antioch in 1051, noticed how the mountain also kept the early morning sun off parts of the city. Ibn Butlan was impressed by the city's strong-looking double wall, which had a circumference of some twelve miles. The wall climbed up steep parts of the mountain, which seemed astonishing, and had five gates and three hundred and sixty towers. Inside the wall were mills, orchards and gardens, and on his way to the city Ibn Butlan had noticed many villages evidently thriving by supplying Antioch with wheat, barley, olives and flowers. All this trade and fertility meant that the city's bazaars were always crowded and well-stocked. Ibn Butlan had come to Antioch to become a monk, and he noticed teaching and other forms of scholarly activity in the city.

Antioch's wealth, the fertility of the land that surrounded it, and the fact that it could withstand a siege, made it a rich military prize. Founded by one of Alexander the Great's generals, it became Roman, was captured by the Arabs in 637, then by the Byzantines in 969. In 1084, a small Turkish force commanded by a prince called Suleiman crept into the city at night and overran it it three days. This was witnessed and recorded by a monk called Michael, who also saw the disastrous outcome of an attempt by the Antiochenes to sally out of one of the city's gates and attack the Turks. As he watched Suleiman's forces make short work of them, Michael:

> ... thought of the joys and dissipations of the Antiochenes which I had witnessed, their excess of pleasure and amusements, their splendid robes, the crowds riding on gorgeously caparisoned mules and camels at the annual festival of St Barbara, with the governor and leading men.

(quoted in *A Short History of Antioch* by E.S. Bouchier)

The soldiers of the First Crusade did not manage to gain control of Antioch as quickly as the Turks had in 1084. They arrived at the end of 1097 and camped out in front of the city for seven weary months, until news came that a new Turkish force was coming to drive them away. At this point, our friend the Norman giant Bohemond put into operation his plan for a surprise night-attack. He persuaded a man called Firouz to surrender one of the city's towers and let in seven hundred knights. The Crusaders who were left outside the walls simultaneously set about destroying one of the gates and making a breach in one of the walls. More gates were opened by members of the Christian population of the city, and soon the streets were filled with shouting Crusaders, who proceeded to massacre Turks and Christians alike. The Turkish governor, Baghi Sian, managed to escape on a mule, but he was later recognised by some local Christians, and his severed head was sent back to the Crusaders in Antioch.

We have independent evidence that Adelard of Bath visited the city of Antioch some twenty years after it had become the capital of a Crusader principality under the control of the Normans. A Spanish scholar and contemporary of Adelard called John of Seville translated a text called, in Latin, the *Liber Prestigiorum Thebidis*. The original of this had been written by a ninth century Arab mathematician called Thabit ibn Qurra, but John of Seville wrote that part of it had already been translated by Adelard. Crucially, the Spaniard referred to Adelard as an Antiochene.

If Adelard stayed at Antioch long enough to be called an Antiochene, it seems likely that the Englishman was there before both it, and the bridge at Mamistra, were hit by the earthquakes of 1114. If he had been crossing the bridge from west to east on his way to Antioch at this time, he would have arrived in a city of funerals, picking their way through piles of rubble in the streets; and also of panic. After the earthquakes of 1114, the Antiochenes were convinced that the Turks would take advantage of the natural disaster and besiege their city. As they scrambled to rebuild their defensive walls, they would surely have had little time to entertain a wandering English scholar.

Anna Comnena described the Firouz who had betrayed Antioch to the Crusaders as an Armenian who had pretended to convert to Islam. One reason why there were Armenians in places like Antioch at this time is because their own country had been overrun by the Turks. This process had ended in 1064 with the sultan Alp Arslan's savage attack on the magnificent Armenian city of Ani. Thereafter, Armenians were forced to stay put under the heel of the Turks, or find a way to live elsewhere.

The Armenian kingdom of Cilicia in the south-east of Anatolia, parts of which Adelard must have crossed to reach the bridge at Mamistra, had been founded, in part, because of a dog and a man in a bag.

The Armenian king Gagik II had been forced into exile by the Byzantines, but his anger was roused when he heard that Markos, the Greek Orthodox Metropolitan of Caesarea, had named his dog Armen, just to spite the Armenians. Gagik arranged for Markos to be put in a bag with his dog, which had been beaten so cruelly with sticks that it went mad and bit its master to death. In revenge, Gagik was killed in 1079 by three Byzantine brothers – a murder that is supposed to have been witnessed by a prince of the Armenian royal line called Roupen. Roupen founded Armenian Cilicia in part to avenge the old king's death. He fought many battles against the Byzantine Greeks, who laid claim to Cilicia, but at last he established a kingdom to pass on to his son Constantine, who ruled from 1095.

From a military point of view, Cilicia has two contrasting types of terrain – the mountains, covered with forests and riddled with defiles, were easy to defend, especially when the monasteries that were scattered in these lonely places could so easily be converted into fortresses. By contrast, the plains, with their rich cities including Mamistra, were less defensible, and were regularly taken and re-taken. As well as the cities, the ports along the Mediterranean coasts, including Ayas, were major assets.

In his History of Armenia, Vahan Kurkjian insists that when

Roupen began to establish his new Cilician kingdom, the whole region had been so devastated by Arab invasions that what should have been fertile land was almost desert. The remaining Greeks, Syrians and Jews huddled together in ruined cities and did not venture far from their walls, even to till the soil.

In 1097 it was Constantine, the son of Roupen, who welcomed the First Crusaders as they passed through Cilicia on their way to the Holy Land. Constantine saw the Crusaders, led by the Frenchman Godfrey of Bouillon, as possible allies against the Byzantine Greeks, as well as the Turks.

Then as now, Armenian national identity had a great deal to do with the Armenian Church, which had been considered quite separate from the rest of Christendom since the fifth century Council of Chalcedon (another historic city that is now in the modern state of Turkey). At Chalcedon, the Armenians had differed from the other churches over their understanding of the exact nature of Jesus.

In the same way that medieval philosophers argued about universals, medieval theologians debated whether Jesus was wholly divine, wholly human, or some sort of combination of both. One approach to this question, which goes by the name Docetism, has it that the human form of Jesus, that was seen by thousands of people during his short life, was nothing more than an illusion. This is reminiscent of Plato's idea that the world that we perceive with our senses is like a mere shadow.

Many modern Christians probably never think of such questions, but it is easy to see why they preoccupied medieval theologians for centuries. In the early days, pagan followers of gods like Jupiter and Venus were converting to Christianity, and it would have been all too easy for them to think of Jesus as some kind of pagan god who had assumed human form. By contrast, Muslims believe that Allah cannot have any partners or associates in his divinity, and that Jesus was just another prophet of God.

The Armenian Church settled on a position defined as miaphysitism, which stated that Jesus combined both divinity and humanity in one nature. This struck the Byzantine Orthodox Christians, who were notorious for their fondness for theological distinctions, as heretical. Aware that the Latin Church to which many of the Crusaders were devoted had itself split off from Greek Orthodoxy in the Great Schism of 1054, the Armenians greeted the Crusaders as liberators.

In the first flush of the honeymoon period enjoyed by the Armenians and the Crusaders, various Armenian leaders supplied the westerners with food, horses, arms and even men. Vahan Kurkjian asserts that Bohemond and his men could hardly have survived during their siege of Antioch if the Armenians had not helped them. Kurkjian also details the important marriages that took place between the Crusaders and Armenian aristocrats. Constantine, who had been awarded the titles of Comes and Baron by the newcomers, gave his daughter to Joscelin, Count of Edessa; and Baldwin, the brother of Godfrey of Bouillon, married a niece of Constantine's.

The enthusiasm of the Armenians about the newcomers proved to be misplaced. The Crusaders, among them Tancred, Bohemond's warlike nephew, were quite happy to take Cilician towns and cities, so that when Adelard was at Mamistra the city was in Crusader hands, and counted as part of the Crusader Principality of Antioch.

In her 1994 book on Adelard, Louise Cochrane speculates on whether the Englishman stayed at Mamistra after he had managed to escape from the city's shaking bridge. This is possible: although earthquakes are rare indeed in England, Adelard might still have had sense enough to realize that returning west through Armenian Clicia straight after such an event would have been foolhardy. But if he had remained at Mamistra, where he would at least have been in the company of Normans like the ones who had conquered his own country, could he have witnessed the rebuilding of the bridge?

If Adelard had been able to get off the bridge during his earthquake, as he claimed, then it may not have been too badly damaged. Cochrane wonders whether the local builders took this opportunity to use pointed, Gothic arches to replace at least some of the arches in the bridge. Did Adelard, with his interest in geometry, take an interest in these arches, few if any of which would have been standing in his native England at this time? Did he understand that they were stronger and more flexible than the round-topped arches of the twelfth century West, and did he pass on this knowledge when he got home?

Although it seems unlikely that the question will ever be properly settled, it has long been suspected that the technically superior Gothic arch was introduced, or perhaps re-introduced, into Western Europe from the East. In his book *Parentalia*, no less a figure than the architect Christopher Wren insisted on this, in a passage that also showed his knowledge of the cultural debt Europe owed to Islam in areas other than architecture:

> If anyone doubts of this assertion, let us appeal to any one who has seen the mosques and palaces of Fez, or some of the cathedrals in Spain, built by the Moors: one model of this sort is the church of Burgos; and even in this island there are not wanting several examples of the same: such buildings have been vulgarly called Modern Gothic, but their true appellation is Arabic, Saracenic, or Moresque . . . learning flourished among the Arabian all the time that their dominion was in full power; they studied philosophy, mathematics, physics, and poetry. The love of learning was at once excited . . . and such of the Greek authors as they had translated into Arabic, were from thence turned into Latin.

One of Adelard's learned contributions was, of course, to be part of the process of re-introducing Greek texts to the West by translating them from Arabic into Latin.

VI. Italy and Sicily

The Norman giant Bohemond had inherited his striking look from his father, Robert Guiscard (meaning Robert the Cunning). This man had ridden into Italy in 1047 with a tiny band of followers, and fought his way up to become one of the most powerful figures in Europe.

In the same way that the First Crusaders, who included among their number Guiscard's son Bohemond, had been able to take advantage of divisions among the Turks, Guiscard's fellow Normans, who had come to Southern Italy as mercenaries and bandits, were able to profit from the deep divisions that beset that region at the time.

We already know that, coming from the Italian city of Salerno, Adelard may have met up with a sort of Greek sage. When Guiscard first rode into Italy there were still parts of the peninsula where Greeks predominated – these communities were what was left of the Byzantine Empire's Italian outposts. At this time, Italy also boasted many natives of Lombard descent – like the Normans, the Lombards had spread south out of Scandinavia in search of land and loot, and had taken over large parts of Italy by the end of the sixth century.

The political picture in Italy in Adelard's time was further complicated by the fact that the Franks, under Charlemagne, had also overrun the peninsula in the eighth century, and Charlemagne's successors, the Holy Roman Emperors, liked to meddle in Italian affairs from time to time. Meanwhile successive popes, who in those days claimed wide lands and commanded formidable armies, added an extra layer of complication to Italian affairs.

Like the Anglo-Saxons whom the Normans conquered in England in 1066, the Normans in Italy were used as mercenaries by various sides, until they decided that they would rather have their own lands than fight for other people's. Their progress in this regard is beautifully summarised by Edmund Curtis in his book *Roger of Sicily*:

Town after town from Crati to Monte Gargano was falling before the siege-craft of the Normans, which consisted in the simple and effective method of blockading the environs, and starving the people into submission. Thereupon, the place was secured by rampart and trench; a valley once occupied, a Norman castle rose on some impregnable spur of the Apennines; the countless mountain-glens of lower Italy were being steadily occupied by Norman lords and their fighting bands.

In mainland Italy, the Normans were fighting fellow-Christians, although as Latin Christians, theoretically loyal to the Pope, they were supposed to regard the Italian Greeks as heretics. As they conquered the island of Sicily, the Normans found themselves fighting the Muslims who had been in control of that sun-drenched Mediterranean stronghold for more than two hundred years. When they took control, they quickly realised that they had to cooperate with the local Muslims, who knew how to run the place and had been doing so very successfully for so long. What emerged was a kind of polyglot paradise, where cultures, languages and ethnicities fed off each other, against a background of general peace and prosperity.

The 'cash cow' for the twelfth century Sicilian economy is thought to have been the island's wheat exports. Somebody, probably the Muslims, had introduced a hardy, drought-resistant wheat variety that was successfully traded all over the Mediterranean. There were also orchards rich with pears, oranges, and the Sicilian lemons that some say are still the best in the world.

Visiting the island in 1185, the Muslim traveller Ibn Jubayr was amazed by its wealth, fertility and culture, but also distressed that all this was under the control of the Norman infidels. His party was treated with such respect that he feared that some local Muslims might be seduced into abandoning Islam and becoming Christians.

It seems that in the court of the Norman King William II, known as William the Good, many Muslims were employed in various roles, but felt obliged to be discreet about their true faith. Ibn Jubayr tells us that when the king's palace at Palermo was hit by an earthquake, the panicking closet-Muslims began to cry out to Allah for help. King William merely advised them to call on the god most likely to give them comfort.

The twelfth century cultural flowering of Norman Sicily produced one very notable bloom; the Arabic poet Ibn Hamdis. An older contemporary of Adelard of Bath, the Englishman could not have met the poet on Sicily because he had left as a teenager after the fall of the city of Messina in 1072. This allowed him to write, among other verses, poems filled with nostalgic longing for Sicily as it was under the Muslims. These were *qasidas* or odes, and are known as Ibn Hamdis's *Siqilliyyat*, a name based on the Arabic name for Sicily.

One of the *Siqilliyyat* describes an epic wine-drinking bout enjoyed by a young man (clearly the author in disguise) and his companions, whom the poet describes as noble and free, and luminous like stars. This event, which unfolded behind locked doors, seems to have taken place one night in a convent in Sicily, to which the young men were drawn by the fragrance of the dark red wine itself. Reading the poem, one is reminded of the classic British pub 'lock-in', where drinkers are able to sup after the legal opening hours, because the doors of the premises are locked and the drunken session is technically a party held by the licensee for his friends.

As he gets drunker, the brain of the young man at the centre of Ibn Hamdis's poem is assailed by surreal images and associations. As one of the barmaids, who has shining, gem-like hands, pours wine from a wine-skin, the poet imagines that the cup itself is drinking from the wine-skin. The bubbles in the wine seem to him to contain birds, and the smell of the wine is like musk. Once diluted with water, the red wine looks like fire. A familiar trope in Arabic wine-poetry, that calls wine itself 'the daughter of the grape', makes the poet think that by drinking wine he is seducing a virgin. The idea of a race-track gets mixed up with all this, as dark red was supposed to be a good colour for a race-horse, and the young man and his companions seem to be racing through the wine. As the night wears on, there is music, singing and dancing.

The poet recounts how wine and music drove away his sorrow as a young man, but at the beginning of the poem he warns the reader that now, at sixty, he resents having had to make himself an exile from Sicily, and is grieved to think of his fellow-Muslims, forced to live in a place dominated by Christians.

In his history of medieval Sicily, Denis Mack Smith recognises the poetry of the exiled Ibn Hamdis as one of the two great literary achievements that sprang from the island during Norman times. Smith's judgement would certainly be backed up by experts in Arabic poetry, who count Ibn Hamdis among the greatest poets in that language that the Middle Ages produced.

The other achievement that Smith tips his hat to is a project that was completed around 1154, that is to say, some twenty years after the death of Ibn Hamdis, and perhaps a couple of years before the death of Adelard of Bath. This was *The Book of Roger*, a collaboration between King Roger II of Sicily and the Spanish Muslim scientist Mohammed al-Idrisi.

Al-Idrisi's introduction to this book, which Roger himself named *The Delight of Those Who Wish to Travel the World*, describes how, once he had settled his kingdom, the Norman king set about trying to learn everything he could about it, and about other lands. This sounds a little like the English Domesday Book, another Norman king's attempt to inventory exactly what he ruled over, but *The Book of Roger* was more ambitious, being intended as nothing less than a description of the known world.

King Roger had a huge silver globe constructed, onto which was inscribed a map of the world divided up into seven zones or climates. The lines on the globe were based on drawings, and if the version of al-Idrisi's map of the known world that appears in an old Oxford manuscript is anything to go by, Roger's globe cannot have been terribly accurate. The Mediterranean looks comparatively small here, while its islands seem very large. Sicily itself seems to have been severely trimmed around its north-east coast, and is much further from the toe of Italy than modern cartographers would insist that it is. As for Italy, it is shaped more like an arm with a mitten at the end of it than a foot or a boot.

Despite its drawbacks as a mapping project, the text of the *Book of Roger* is the fascinating result of years of research conducted among whatever travellers Roger and al-Idrisi could find and question. These first-hand accounts of every detail of every country possible were put together with the results of interviews with expert geographers, and researches among old books on the subject, including the works of Claudius Ptolemy.

It is hard to imagine a better place than Sicily at that time for sourcing informants on different parts of the world. As well as Lombards, Normans, Greeks, Jews, Arabs and other Muslims from the Middle East, North Africa and Muslim Spain, there must have been people who were either visiting or living on the island who had travelled much further afield as pilgrims, traders or Crusaders.

Their twelfth-century focus groups and other sources told Roger and his tame geographer about black people in Africa who wore no clothes and produced very large numbers of children, and the women of Nubia, who were reported to be ravishingly beautiful. The island of Socotra, off the north-east coast of Africa, was said to be full of Christians because Alexander the Great had replaced the natives with a Greek colony, which turned Christian shortly after the coming of Jesus.

According to the *Book of Roger*, Alexander also reached Spain (in fact he never went further west than Greece) and, finding the Mediterranean cut off from the Atlantic, caused a huge canal to be dug to link the two seas and equalise their water-levels. If this is true, then the Straits of Gibraltar should be called the Straits of Alexander.

The *Book of Roger* also describes cannibals living in Borneo and Malaysia, and the seven castes into which Indians were born. Al-Idrisi also explains how intelligent elephants are, and how China is ruled by a Buddhist 'King of Kings' called the Bagh-

Bûgh. England, which is not recognisable on al-Idrisi's map, is described as having a shape like the head of an ostrich, and also as fertile and full of brave and enterprising people. Unfortunately, these people are forced to live in a perpetual winter, while, further north, the Scots have no towns, villages or even houses.

A key piece of evidence that suggests that Adelard of Bath visited Sicily is his dedication of *On the Same and the Different* to William, Bishop of Syracuse (Syracuse is an ancient city in the eastern part of Sicily, which is one of the places apparently trimmed off in al-Idrisi's world map). In his dedication, Adelard describes Bishop William as 'most learned in all the mathematical arts', and in his book on the twelfth-century English exchequer, Poole suggests that this bishop might have been the mysterious 'William R' to whom an Englishman called Turchill dedicated his book on the abacus.

In her book on Adelard, Louise Cochrane entertains the possibility that the Bathonian's travels among the Muslims consisted only of a long stay on Sicily, and that he was never seen in the other places he claims to have been – Cilicia and Antioch. Cochrane dismisses this as unlikely, but it *is* likely that various places in relatively peaceful, prosperous Sicily would have been more convenient for Adelard the student than turbulent Cilicia and Antioch. There the rulers, Norman or otherwise, were more like war-lords than kings, and the ever-present threat of conflict meant that the pursuit of learning and culture became a secondary concern.

In Sicily, Adelard would have been able to find towns, villages and parts of cities where he could have immersed himself in Muslim culture, attending Muslim schools, consulting Arabic texts and conversing with sheikhs and scholars. Even if his spoken Arabic was imperfect, many of his Sicilian Muslim contacts would probably have been able to converse with him in Greek, Latin or even Norman French. In the province of Trapani, at a place Ibn Jubayr calls Hisn al-Hammah, the Bathonian would also have been able to see the familiar sight of natural hot springs.

VII. Natural Questions

The *Natural Questions* is the longest of Adelard's original works, i.e. the longest that was not a translation or adaptation: nevertheless, it only takes up some seventy pages in English translation. Like his earlier book *On the Same and the Different*, *Natural Questions* is supposedly intended as a teaching text for Adelard's unnamed nephew. One difference is that the longer text, in which Adelard reveals that seven years have passed since he wrote the first, is set out as a dialogue with his nephew, rather than a text addressed to the boy.

As the name might suggest, *Natural Questions* revolves around a series of questions put to Adelard by his nephew during their dialogue. There are seventy-six of these, and some of them were already old (one might even say they were old chestnuts) by the time Adelard turned to them. The questions themselves concern the natural world, so that Charles Burnett calls them 'questions on natural science' in his 1998 English translation.

The twelfth century Western European intellectual mindset meant that when Adelard and his nephew discuss such subjects as animals, plants, light, the five senses and the human brain, they bring in theological speculations about the nature of the soul, the role, nature and intentions of the Creator, and the shape and nature of the universe. This must be disconcerting for any reader who opens Adelard's *Natural Questions* expecting to read a 'purely' scientific text. As in his *On the Same and the Different*, Adelard is trying not to break up knowledge into discrete fragments – he is trying to find unity – the medieval version of the modern 'Theory of Everything'.

Natural Questions is a true dialogue, in that here Adelard's nephew is not content merely to sit at his uncle's feet, politely offering him a series of questions and meekly accepting his replies. Sometimes he admits to deliberately concocting questions intended to annoy his uncle, and many of his supplementary questions show that he is not prepared to accept his uncle's initial answers. At times, the nephew seems determined to test his uncle's answers to destruction, but, since Adelard is the author of the piece as well as being one of the voices in it, he tends to get the last word.

Sometimes the two participants in the dialogue seem to be genuinely exasperated with each other, and they trade insults as well as ideas. Underlying much of what the nephew says is his feeling, which evidently has not diminished during the seven years since *On the Same and the Different*, that his uncle's habit of travelling all over the known world in search of knowledge is not a good habit. The young man also seems to be convinced that, since they are not Christians, the Arabs may have misled Adelard. For his part, Adelard characterises the French learning his nephew has been absorbing as insecure ('*inconstantiam*' in the original Latin).

The uncle's concern is that his nephew's French masters may have instilled in him too great a respect for the ideas and opinions of the great authorities of the past. Implying that this is part of what the Arabs taught him, Adelard insists on the application of reason as well as authority to questions about nature.

Unfortunately, both the ancient authorities Adelard and his nephew discuss, the reasoning Adelard applies to many of the questions, and even some of the questions themselves are based on science that a modern child of twelve would find fault with, if the modern child had received a half-decent education up to that age. Adelard's answers are, however, elegant and even poetic. They reveal the way the twelfth century mind worked, and they show that what the scientists of the time lacked in the way of experimental evidence, they could sometimes make up for with thinking and observation.

A perfect example of how most of *Natural Questions* works as a book can be found in the author's treatment of the first question, which asks how plants manage to grow without any seed being sown. Any gardener will be familiar with this phenomenon – in the midst of a neat bed of blooms specially planted or sown, an unwanted plant appears, as if by magic. This 'plant in the wrong place' is called a weed. Today we know that such unexpected plants grow from seeds that have got into the soil by accident. In the Middle Ages, many still believed that they grew from nothing – by a process called spontaneous generation. Flies that hatched out from rotten meat were also thought to originate from the same process; and in Shakespeare's *Antony and Cleopatra* a very drunk Lepidus describes how Egyptian snakes and crocodiles were thought to come into existence: 'Your serpent of Egypt is bred now of your mud by the operation of your sun. So is your crocodile' (Act 2, scene 7).

Adelard's nephew reminds him that plants even spring up from soil that has been carefully sieved to extract any stray seeds. How can this be? The questioner is also puzzled as to how a plant, a living thing that must therefore be made up of the four elements of water, air, fire and earth, can grow out of something that is, by definition, just earth (in the Middle Ages, it was believed that everything was made up of these four elements).

In his reply, Adelard asserts that the earth that seems to utter spontaneous growth is not pure earth, but has to have had some traces of water, air and fire as well. This is reminiscent of Adelard's thoughts on the vexed question of the nature of universals in his earlier book *On the Same and the Different*. There he asserted that things themselves, properly observed, were found to contain within them characteristics that linked them to the universal idea behind them. Remember our example of Bohemond, who displayed so many unusual and even unique qualities, but also contained enough of the general, abstract idea of a man to be recognised as a man without hesitation. In his *Natural Questions*, Adelard seems to be implying that though the pure, abstract idea of earth could never sustain a plant, the impure earth of the real world can. In fact he says that no one will ever experience pure air, water, earth or fire in the natural world.

By reason and observation, Adelard shows how a plant that

appears by spontaneous generation exhibits its combined nature, which necessarily consists of all four elements. It springs upwards like fire, reaching out into the air, and spreads out horizontally like water spilled on the floor; and of course it grows out of the earth.

Adelard's ability to see all four elements in a simple plant reminds us of Ibn Hamdis's ability to see, with his poet's eye, fire in red wine. As well as being poetic, Adelard's account of the spontaneous growth of plants reflects his typically twelfth century view of the universe – a universe that is so teeming with life that it can even spring from nothing and in which, as Adelard also asserts in the *Natural Questions*, the planets themselves are regarded as animate beings.

The planets must be living things possessing some kind of consciousness, Adelard argues, because they change their courses in the sky and do not travel in straight lines or predictable curves, like many other stars (in fact our word 'planet' comes from an old Greek word meaning 'wanderer', because of the planets' wandering habits). Adelard is forced to come to this conclusion because the apparent wandering of the planets cannot be adequately explained by the Ptolomaic model, which places the Earth at the centre of the universe.

In his explanation of how eyesight works, Adelard also makes it clear that the science of his time regarded all the important elements of the universe as visible to the naked eye. The fiery, invisible beams that were supposed to shoot out from the eyes can stretch to the *aplanos*, the furthest of the interlocking spheres to which the stars are attached, and therefore the very edge of the universe and the most distant thing that could ever be seen. By contrast, modern ideas give us a universe that seems to stretch endlessly in every direction, much of which can never be seen.

The question about the spontaneous growth of plants is based on what we now know to be a false premise, as is question number forty-one, which concerns, of all things, the sexual transmission of leprosy. Why, asks the nephew, does a woman who has sex with a leper not catch the disease, but passes it on to the next man she has sex with? As in the question about the spontaneous growth of plants, Adelard resorts to the theory of the four elements to answer this one. The disease cannot take hold of the woman because women are naturally more cold and moist than men. Men, by contrast, are hot and dry, and their bodies are therefore a better breeding-ground for the infection.

It is hard to imagine how the people of Adelard's time could have concluded that women could be 'carriers' of leprosy, much as Typhoid Mary was found to be a deadly carrier of typhoid, but displayed no symptoms of the disease, in the early years of the twentieth century. It may be that this medieval misconception arose from the fact that leprosy is not sexually transmitted, and that infected people can go for years, even decades, without showing any symptoms. Perhaps the rumour arose because of a case of a woman who was known to have had sex with a leper, whose next sexual partner developed symptoms soon after their encounter. The second man could have been infected for up to twenty years, but by chance only started to notice symptoms soon after his time with the unfortunate woman in the story.

Their discussion of women, sex and leprosy leads Adelard and his nephew onto the subject of women in general. Their 'temperament' (the mix or 'temper' of the four elements in their natures) means that they are naturally more lecherous than men; and, since opposites attract, their moistness and coldness means that they are naturally attracted to the hotness and dryness of men.

Adelard also resorts to the idea of the four elements in his explanation of thunder and lightning. The sound of thunder, he asserts, is caused when vast sheets of ice, which form in the clouds, are smashed up. Lightning comes because, like the earth in the question about plants, the water from which the ice is formed is not 'pure' water: it has traces of the other three elements in it as well. When it breaks, the fire in it is suddenly released, in the form of lightning. This explanation also yields an explanation of the hail and rain that can sometimes fall during or after a thunder-storm. The hail is what is left of the shattered sheets of ice – but this lands as rain if it is melted by warm air on the way down.

The man from Bath resorts to philosophy rather than the pseudo-scientific idea of the four elements in his answer to his nephew's most whimsical query, which tackles the question of why humans don't have horns on their heads. Other animals have such weapons, the young man argues; either horns, or teeth, or claws. Why are humans so defenceless, when they are constantly making war against each other?

In his answer, Adelard reminds his nephew that human beings have the brains to make weapons for themselves, for instance out of wood and metal, when they need them, which is why they don't need horns as a permanent weapon. They also have the power to make peace and lay down those man-made weapons: a bull, by contrast, cannot lay down his horns.

Still in the area of the human head, Adelard's nephew asks how the ancient philosophers, including Aristotle, found out that the imagination is seated in the front part of the brain, the reason in the middle, and memory at the back. This is another question based on a false premise, since the brain is not divided up in that way; but it is still an interesting question because it is what we might call a 'how do they know that?' question. Such questions are surely more advanced than the simple 'why' questions that, for instance, small children will ask. Questioning how a piece of knowledge was established reveals some understanding, on the part of the questioner, of how knowledge and learning work in themselves.

The educated guess Adelard uses to answer this question does not rely on observation or the theory of the four elements, and seems truly scientific and modern. Surely, he suggests, this knowledge was built up by the ancients on the basis of reports of cases of people who had survived injuries to the brain. By testing and questioning such people, Adelard implies, impairments could be discovered; so that a man who had lost part of the front part of his brain lost all imagination, whereas a man who had lost part of the back of his brain had trouble remembering things.

In fact people who have survived major brain injuries have proved invaluable to scientists trying to work out which part of the brain does what. They were particularly useful in the days before x-rays and more high-tech modern scans. The idea that a brain injury might affect behaviour was brought home to the medical world by the case of Phineas Gage, an American railway worker who lost a large part of the front of his brain (as well as the sight of his left eye) when a thick metal spike was accidentally shot right through his head in 1848. Adelard, and indeed Aristotle, might have been disappointed to learn that Gage's imagination seems not to have been affected by this. In fact he seems to have become more imaginative, forever cooking up hare-brained schemes to get rich. It was Gage's personality and social behaviour that deteriorated: J.M. Harlow, the doctor who first attended to Gage's wounds, reported that he had become 'fitful, irreverent, indulging at times in the grossest profanity (which was not previously his custom), manifesting but little deference for his fellows' and 'impatient of restraint or advice.'

Another 'how do they know that?' question that Adelard's nephew poses in the *Natural Questions* concerns human anatomy. How did the ancient philosophers know that there were nerves and blood-vessels in the body, when such things were likely to be destroyed as soon as the body was cut open in order to examine them?

Here, as elsewhere in the *Natural Questions*, Adelard refers to his travels in order to answer the question. He tells his nephew that he discussed this very subject with a man in Tarsus in Cilicia, the birthplace of Saint Paul (close to Mamistra, where Adelard found himself on the shaking bridge).

This unnamed man of Tarsus is another of the anonymous wise men whom Adelard is supposed to have consulted during his travels. First there was the expert on astronomy who appeared at the start of *On the Same and the Different*, then there was the man in Magna Graecia who appeared at the end of that book, and in *Natural Questions* Adelard tells us about a man from Tarsus.

From this last anonymous donor of wisdom Adelard learned that there was once a grisly experiment designed to lay bare the nerves and blood-vessels of the human body without recourse to the dissector's knife. A cadaver was lowered into a river and tied up in such a way that it could not be dislodged and carried downstream. Over time, the current wore away the body's outer skin and fat, revealing the networks of nerves and vessels beneath the surface.

VIII. Glimpses of a Life

There are hints, like blood-vessels or nerves lying below the skin of some of the autobiographical details in *Natural Questions*, which suggest that Adelard may have been just a little bit insufferable on his return from his travels. In the main body of the *Natural Questions*, it is clear that Adelard's nephew is already weary of his uncle's attempts to promote the scientific approach of the Arabs. In the book's dedication, to Richard, Bishop of Bayeux, the author pours scorn on the country to which he has returned, saying that the local princes are barbarous, the bishops heavy drinkers, the judges susceptible to bribery, and everybody else dishonest and grasping.

In response to this sorry state of affairs, Adelard thinks about giving up on his own people, but then decides to try to improve matters by writing his *Natural Questions*, so that at least the benighted English will have a chance to benefit from the wisdom of the Arabs. Of course this is very condescending, and implies that the traveller did not encounter hypocrisy, drunkenness or overweening ambition in Sicily, Cilicia or the Principality of Antioch; which seems unlikely.

Travellers who return full of annoying ideas have long been figures of fun for the English. In Shakespeare's *As You Like It*, Rosalind reminds the melancholy Jaques, whom she identifies as a traveller, of the behaviour expected of natives who have returned from foreign lands:

Look you lisp and wear strange suits, disable all the benefits of your own country, be out of love with your nativity, and almost chide God for making you that countenance you are, or I will scarce think you have swam in a gondola.

(Act 4, scene 1)

Rosalind's mention of a gondola suggests that Shakespeare has in mind travellers who have returned from an early version of the Grand Tour, which would often include a trip to Venice. In the eighteenth century, men who returned from Italy who lisped and wore 'strange suits' were called macaronis because of their fondness for that type of pasta. Later London, and indeed Bath, had to put up with the notorious English 'nabobs', who had become rich through working for the East India Company, and were determined to live in England like emperors rather than upstart merchants. Within living memory, the English have also had to smile indulgently at the 'hippy' travellers who returned from India with a strong tendency to sit cross-legged on the floor (even when there were plenty of chairs available) and a conviction that the Sub-Continent was somehow more 'real' than, say, Surbiton.

It is possible that Adelard of Bath wore 'strange suits' like Rosalind's archetypal traveller. In the *Natural Questions*, he lets slip that he is wearing a green cloak and an emerald ring. Were these items acquired in a bazaar at Antioch or on Sicily? Did they make the man from Bath stand out like an exotic popinjay among his Western European associates?

Adelard may have regarded his emerald ring as a stylish accessory that also possessed magical powers. His older French contemporary Marbodius of Rennes wrote that emeralds could give their wearers the power to see into the future, speak persuasively, calm storms and even cure illnesses.

The most startling autobiographical detail that emerges from the *Natural Questions* is a brief account of a visit Adelard and his nephew paid to an elderly sorceress, to learn about her spells. They appear to have stayed with this lady for several days, but the thing about the visit that stuck in the nephew's mind was a gadget used by the old lady's 'water steward' to dispense water so that her guests could wash their hands at the dinner-table. Did this work by magic? the nephew asks.

Adelard assures the young man that this curious device was not in fact magic: although long-winded and partly theoretical, the uncle's explanation shows that it worked like an elaborate pipette or eye-dropper with multiple openings. The fact that she was able to afford such a gadget, employed a steward who was responsible for its use, and was also able to provide bed and board for Adelard and his nephew suggests that their hospitable sorceress was a woman of substance; but how she got her money, who she was and even where she lived are unknown.

Although he realised that the water-dispenser he saw in the sorceress's house was not magical, Adelard still had an interest in magic or, to be more precise, he was unable to distinguish science from what we would now call mumbo-jumbo. In this, he was absolutely typical of the thinkers of his time.

Among Abelard's surviving works on magic is the aforementioned translation of an Arabic book known in Latin as the *Liber Prestigiorum* of Thabit ibn Qurra. Thabit was a ninth-century Arab scientist born in Harran, another ancient city in what is now Turkey; in this case in the south-east of Anatolian Turkey. Although he was an Arab, Thabit's first language was Syriac, which is related to the Aramaic that Jesus would have spoken. Also fluent in both Greek and Arabic, Thabit lived and worked in Baghdad, then a major centre of learning and culture. Although surrounded by Muslims, Thabit stuck to his Sabean religion – an ancient faith, mentioned several times in the Qur'an, about which little is now known.

Adelard's translation of the *Liber Prestigiorum* is concerned with the use of inscribed amulets to garner magical powers from the stars and other heavenly bodies. Although the inscriptions described can be scratched into gem-stones, Thabit insists that almost anything will do, including sheets of lead and balls of mud. What is important is that the drawings, letters and symbols are inscribed correctly, and that every part of the procedure is done at the correct time. The timing is determined by careful observation of the heavens, or, if that is not possible, by consulting astronomical tables. With the powers thus assembled, the adept will be able to, for instance, become a king's favourite, re-heat the love of a cooling spouse, reduce a city to rubble, recover stolen treasure, start a war, win a lawsuit or become rich.

Once the amulets, whatever they are made of, are inscribed correctly, and at exactly the right time, Adelard recommends that they are smoked or 'suffumigated' with the wood of aloe, saffron and balsam if good is intended, and red sandalwood and resin if evil is intended – for instance if the adept is trying to sow discord between two friends.

The amulet thus made and lightly smoked should be buried, again at exactly the right time, while certain incantations are uttered. All this must be done with confidence – any hesitation might cause the spell to fail or misfire. If the amulet is supposed to bring round a reluctant lover, it should be buried under the doorway of his or her house. If it is supposed to, for instance, destroy a city, it should be buried in the middle of the city. The blood or body-parts of certain animals might be required at this point.

It is hardly surprising that some twelfth century thinkers regarded this sort of thing as demonic. The German philosopher, theologian and bishop Albertus Magnus, a younger contemporary of Adelard's, put the Bathonian's *Liber Prestigiorum* right at the top of his list of abominable books. He particularly objected to Adelard's 'suffumigations', which he felt transformed his book from a scientific volume into a text about evil spirits.

It is hard to say how seriously Adelard took all this. The *Liber Prestigiorum* is certainly not his only magical text or translation, though scholars are unsure how many others can be attributed to him. It seems that his sense of humour got the better of him when he came to translating Thabit's recipe for ridding the city of Baghdad of scorpions. He substituted the name of his home town, Bath, for that of Baghdad, and proceeded to explain how to drive all the scorpions out of an English city where such creatures are never met with.

To rid Bath of scorpions, first one must create an image of a scorpion curled up backwards as if stinging itself. This must share its amulet with other inscriptions of an astrological nature, for which the adept will need to know the names of such things as 'the lord of the ascendant' and 'the lord of the hour'. The amulet should then be buried in the middle of the city, while the adept recites certain magic words. All this should happen when the moon is in Scorpio.

If any readers are tempted to try this because they believe that there may be one or two scorpions lurking in Bath's Georgian masonry, they should remember that if certain parts of the procedure are done incorrectly, innumerable scorpions will be magically drawn to the city.

To work properly, the spells in Adelard's *Liber Prestigiorum* require the adept to have a detailed and accurate knowledge of the movements of the stars and planets, especially as they relate to the signs of the zodiac. If some twelfth century mage living in, say, Provence, where scorpions are common, wanted to rid his city of them, his efforts might have been frustrated by clouds that made it impossible for him to identify 'the lord of the ascendant', 'the lord of the hour' and the position of the moon. In that case, he might have done well to turn to another translation of Adelard's: of the astronomical tables of the aforementioned al-Khwarizmi. If the Provençal wizard had a clear view of the heavens, and also had an astrolabe to hand, he might also have found a use for Adelard's treatise on that scientific instrument.

Adelard's translation of al-Khwarizmi's tables was useful for astrological purposes beyond those detailed in the Bathonian's book on the use of magical amulets. It could also be used to cast horoscopes, and some now believe that ten English horoscopes that have survived from the middle of the twelfth century may be Adelard's own work. These were drawn up for royal clients, which would suggest that, if they are his, the Bathonian was moving in very exalted circles, at least when he reached his seventies. It may be that Adelard had a handy point of contact with the less intellectual and more sport-oriented members of the royal court thanks to his *Tractate on Birds*, a short work on falconry.

Being a figure in the royal court was not entirely risk-free at this time, and the reasons for this went beyond the drunkenness and corruption that Adelard had noticed among his countrymen when he returned to England. This was the reign of King Stephen – the only Stephen who ever sat on the English throne. It was time of chaos, anarchy and civil war, caused in part by the king's shaky claim to the crown. When Adelard may have been drawing up his royal horoscopes, the great question was whether Stephen would be succeeded by his own son, Eustace, or Henry, the son of the Empress Matilda, the daughter whom Stephen's predecessor, King Henry I, had named as his heir.

Adelard, or whoever drew up one of the royal horoscopes from this time, was tasked with using the stars to predict whether or not Matilda's son Henry would come to England. In the event he did, and became King Henry II, thanks to a treaty he had made with Stephen at Winchester in 1153. Whatever Adelard's loyalties had been during the civil war that was ended by this treaty, it is likely that the Bathonian was delighted to see the new Henry on the throne, if he lived until 1154 to witness the coronation. Adelard may have tutored Henry in mathematics, and probably dedicated his treatise on the astrolabe to the young prince.

IX. The Greatest Bathonian?

I first came across Adelard of Bath in a footnote in a book about the ancient Library of Alexandria, remembered as one of the greatest libraries that has ever existed. The footnote related that Adelard, called 'Athelard' here, had translated Euclid's *Elements*, the archetypal book on geometry, and surely one of the most successful text-books ever written. Euclid, who is sometimes called Euclid of Alexandria, flourished around 300 BC, and probably used and worked in the great library.

Unfortunately, the author of the book on the Alexandrian Library used his footnote to relate that 'Athelard' had studied Arabic science and culture by travelling in disguise to the Muslim part of Spain. It seems that the jury is still out on the issue of whether Adelard ever went to Spain, but during my research for this book I have not been able to find any hints of his donning any disguises.

Although he may not have been the twelfth century version of an industrial spy, Adelard of Bath could hardly have had a more interesting or varied career. It is unfortunate that we still know so little about him, and that some of what we think we know is based on conjecture. Did he really write those ten royal horoscopes from the middle of the twelfth century? Is that treatise on palmistry his? When he dedicated his treatise on the astrolabe to 'the king's grandson', did he really mean the future King Henry II? Did he really travel as far afield as he claimed?

Enough is known about Adelard for the prestigious Bath Literary and Scientific Institution, based in Queen Square, to champion him with conferences, some well-judged web-pages and their own edition of Louise Cochrane's book. In the 'brief synopsis' that appears on the Institution's handsome website, Michael Davis flirts with the idea that Adelard may be 'our greatest Bathonian', and laments the fact that due to 'a strange case of civic amnesia' Bath seems to have forgotten him. Davis identifies one possible reason for this – that people know about Georgian Bath and Roman Bath, but not about medieval Bath.

It seems that certain times become attached to certain places. It is unlikely, for instance, that the little town of Woodstock in the state of New York will ever shake off the reputation it acquired after a famous music festival happened nearby in the summer of 1969. Also in the musical field, it may be that Vienna was never quite so Viennese as when Johann Strauss was living there and writing and conducting his celebrated waltzes. While some foreign visitors might feel vaguely disappointed that London no longer has choking smogs or Hansom cabs, the noses of most Bath-bound tourists would surely be put out of joint if they were not able to see traces of the Georgian period there, however fake. To them, the city belongs to Jane Austen and Beau Nash, neither of whom were born there, or even in Somerset (in fact Nash was born in Wales).

Adelard should be remembered, and not just by modern Bathonians and visitors to Bath, as a man who formed a sort of human bridge between the science and culture of the Arabs and those of the West. His work, like that of many western Arabists who followed in his footsteps, was important because Arabic science and culture was far superior to the science and culture of the West throughout much of the medieval period (in his 'brief synopsis' Michael Davis claims that in Adelard's day the Arabs were eight hundred years ahead of the Christian West).

Part of the twelfth-century superiority of Arabic culture was founded on the work of Muslim scholars based in cities like Palermo, Cordova and Baghdad who strove to recover, translate, write commentaries and even improve on texts from the ancient Greeks and Romans that had been lost to the West. At Laon in France, star-gazing by the River Loire, Adelard had the insight to see that by travelling east he might learn something quite extraordinary, not just about another culture, but about the long-lost fragments of his own. As works like Adelard's *Natural Questions* show us, the two cultures turned out to have a great deal in common.

Today, as in the twelfth century, the metaphorical bridge between the Western and Muslim worlds sometimes seems as shaky as the bridge at Mamistra on which Adelard experienced his earthquake in 1114. Although over two and a half million Muslims now live in the UK, many of their non-Muslim neighbours know very little about Muslim religion, culture or history. Against this background, anyone who dares to venture across the bridge between the two worlds is an heir of Adelard.

Select Bibliography

Aakhus, Patricia: *Astral Magic and Adelard of Bath's Liber Prestigiorum; or Why Werewolves Change at the Full Moon,* Culture and Cosmos, Vol. 16 nos. 1 and 2, 2012, pp. 151-161
Arnold, Thomas and Guillaume, Alfred: *The Legacy of Islam,* Oxford, 1931
Barber, Malcolm: *The Crusader States,* Yale, 2012
Billings, Malcolm: *The Cross and the Crescent,* BBC, 1987
Boethius: *The Consolation of Philosophy,* Penguin, 1999
Bouchier E. S.: *A Short History of Antioch 300 B.C.-A.D. 1268,* Oxford, 1921
Broadhurst, R.J.C. (trans.): *The Travels of Ibn Jubayr,* Jonathan Cape, 1952
Burnett, Charles (trans.): *Adelard of Bath: Conversations With His Nephew,* Cambridge, 1998
Cochrane, Louise: *Adelard of Bath,* British Museum, 1994
Cresswell, Paul (ed.): *Bath in Quotes,* Ashgrove, 1985
Curtis, Edmund: Roger of Sicily, *Putnam's,* 1912
Duby, Georges: *The Early Growth of the European Economy,* Weidenfeld & Nicolson, 1974
Erickson, Carolly: *Brief Lives of the English Monarchs,* Constable, 2007
Filian, George H.: *Armenia and Her People,* American Publishing Company, 1896
Flower, D.A.: *The Shores of Wisdom,* Pharos, 1999
Haskins, C.H.: *The Renaissance of the Twelfth Century,* Harvard, 1971
Hinde, Thomas: *Tales from the Pump Room,* Gollancz, 1988
Kurkjian, Vahan M. *A History of Armenia,* Armenian General Benevolent Union of America, 1958
Mack Smith, Denis: *Medieval Sicily,* Chatto & Windus, 1968
Maimonides, Moses: *The Guide for the Perplexed,* Dover, 2000
Mallette, Karla: *The Kingdom of Sicily, 1100-1250; A Literary History,*

University of Pennsylvania Press, 2005
Noll, Mark A.: *Turning Points*, Baker Academic, 2012
Norwich, John Julius: *The Normans in the South*, Longmans, 1967
Ordericus Vitalis: *The Ecclesiastical History of England and Normandy*, Bohn, 1854
Poole, Reginald: *The Exchequer in the Twelfth Century*, Oxford, 1912
Poole, Reginald: *Illustrations of the History of Medieval Thought in the Departments of Theology and Ecclesiastical Politics*, Williams and Norgate, 1884
Runciman, Steven: *A History of the Crusades Volume I*, Penguin, 1965
Runciman, Steven: *A History of the Crusades Volume II*, Penguin, 1965
Russell, Bertrand: *History of Western Philosophy*, George Allen and Unwin, 1946
Sewter, E.R.A. (trans.): *The Alexiad of Anna Comnena*, Penguin, 1969
Sweetenham, Carol (trans.): *Robert the Monk's History of the First Crusade*, Ashgate, 2005
Watkins, Carl: Stephen: *The Reign of Anarchy, Penguin*, 2015
Yewdale, Ralph Bailey: *Bohemond I, Prince of Antioch*, Princeton, 1917

For free downloads and more from the Langley Press,
please visit our website at: http://tinyurl.com/lpdirect

Made in the USA
Middletown, DE
03 November 2023

41931926R00043